THE 6 LINES

ONE STORY. ONE SAVIOR.

YUSUPH EMMANUEL

First edition, 2026

ISBN: 979-8-9951700-1-3

Cover and interior design by Kayla Ferman

Published by Yusuph Emmanuel

Printed in the United States of America

To my God—

who found me when I was lost,
who rescued me,
who sustains me,
and keeps me.

To my family—

who carries me with steadfast, unrelenting love.

To my brother Boaz—

whose life,
and whose absence,
still shape my steps.

To the Church—

Christ's redeemed people,
bearing His light into
places it has not yet reached.

And to the world Jesus came,
bled, and rose to save—

This is for you

TABLE OF CONTENTS

"But God shows his love for us in that while we were still sinners, Christ died for us."

ROMANS 5:8

A HOLY INTERRUPTION

I did not come to church that morning expecting anything unusual. It was an ordinary Sunday—November 16, 2025. I walked in carrying nothing remarkable, just a quiet heart ready to listen. I sat in my usual place as my pastor, Adam Griffin, continued our Family of God series.

The message centered on offerings and ordinances—faithful, steady, biblical teaching. Nothing pointed toward evangelism. Nothing hinted at sketches, tools, or anything remotely connected to what was about to unfold inside me. And yet, somewhere in the middle of the sermon, a quiet shift took place.

It wasn't emotional or dramatic, and it wasn't connected to anything Pastor Adam said. It felt deeper—an unmistakable stirring of the Holy Spirit. Over the years, I've learned to recognize those moments when God interrupts, not with noise or urgency, but with clarity. And in that stillness, a single thought entered my mind with surprising weight:

What if there were a simpler way to share the gospel?

It was just one sentence—soft, unforced—yet it carried the kind of weight that slows your heart, as if heaven itself were pressing gently on your shoulders and whispering, *Pay attention.* It felt less like an idea forming and more like something being entrusted.

Before I realized what I was doing, I reached for my notebook. I wasn't brainstorming or trying to create something new. I was simply responding—listening, following, obeying. I drew two lines, then two more, and then two more—six lines in total.

As those simple strokes formed on the page, something began to emerge—something I had never seen before, yet something that felt instantly familiar. A story told through six lines, revealing three movements: brokenness, redemption, and worship—a visual expression of the gospel—clear, complete, and accessible to anyone.

Almost immediately, doubt followed.

The world already has countless gospel tools. Who am I to add another? Does anyone really need a new diagram? Why would God give this to me?

I nearly closed the notebook. Part of me questioned the value of the moment. Part of me wondered if I was imagining it. Part of me felt unworthy to hold anything that might help others explain the gospel.

Yet beneath those questions was a deeper peace—steady, grounding, unmistakable. The thought did not drift away. It remained quiet but persistent. Not urgent, but intentional

And so I kept drawing. I kept writing. I kept listening. The longer I sat with those six lines, the more I realized their simplicity was not a weakness but their strength.

Anyone could draw them: a child in a schoolyard, a teenager explaining faith to a friend, a grandmother in a remote Tanzanian village sharing Christ from her yard, a pastor teaching a congregation with or without a whiteboard. Any believer, anywhere, could carry the gospel in six strokes of a pen.

I didn't yet understand the full weight of what was unfolding, but I recognized God's fingerprints. It reminded me of how He so often works throughout Scripture—meeting His people in ordinary places and interrupting routine moments with eternal purpose.

A bush that burned without being consumed (Exodus 3).
A voice calling in the night (1 Samuel 3).
A vision on a rooftop (Acts 10).
A blinding light on the road to Damascus (Acts 9).

This was not a strategy, a brand, or a polished method. It was a whisper—a small revelation from a big God. And in His hands, small revelations often travel farther than we imagine.

I walked out of church that morning carrying something I had not brought in. I didn't know where it would lead, who it would reach, or how it would be used. I only knew that God had given me something I could not ignore.

This book is simply the result of saying yes to that holy interruption—and trusting God with what He chooses to do next.

WHY THIS STORY MATTERS

Most believers genuinely want to share their faith. They care about people, they love Jesus, and they hope their lives reflect the hope they've received. Yet for many, sharing the gospel still feels intimidating. We fear not knowing enough, saying too much, or creating awkwardness. The result is hesitation—not because we lack conviction, but because we lack confidence.

We live in a time of unprecedented access to information and unprecedented confusion. There are more sermons than ever before, more podcasts, more books, more debates, and more opinions. And yet, in many places, there is less clarity.

Many believers love Jesus deeply but feel unsure how to explain why. The gospel has not lost its power—but in our minds, it has grown complicated.

This book was not written to add another layer of complexity. It was written to remove it.

The gospel is not fragile. It does not depend on impressive vocabulary or flawless delivery. It is not sustained by eloquence.

It stands on truth. And truth, when spoken clearly, carries its own authority.

At its core, the Christian message is not a scattered set of doctrines but a unified story—the story of a good God, a broken world, a redeeming Savior, and a restored purpose. It explains why we ache, why we hope, why we long for justice, and why forgiveness moves us so deeply. It makes sense of both suffering and joy.

Yet many Christians have been handed fragments without a framework. We know verses but struggle to see the arc. We know truths but aren't sure how they fit together. When someone asks, "What do Christians actually believe?" we feel pressure to say everything at once—and fear saying it imperfectly.

The six lines were born from a simple conviction: The gospel can be remembered, carried, and shared as one coherent story. They are a visual framework—six simple strokes—that trace the movement of Scripture from brokenness to redemption to restored purpose.

They are not a replacement for Scripture or a shortcut around theology. They are not a technique to master. They are a tool to help you hold the story steadily in your mind so you can offer it with confidence and compassion.

If you are a pastor... these pages may serve your teaching and discipleship.

If you are a parent... they may help you explain the gospel to your children.

If you are a new believer... they may give you language for the hope you've found.

If you have followed Jesus for decades but still feel hesitant to speak... they may steady your hands.

The goal is not that you would memorize a diagram, but that you would remember the story clearly enough to share it—in a hospital room, across a kitchen table, on a bus ride, or in a brief conversation while standing in line.

This book exists because of a simple truth: The gospel is powerful not because we present it perfectly, but because it is true, and because God is the One who saves.

Before we turn to the story of how God shaped my life and calling, I want to invite you into the purpose of these pages: to rediscover the clarity of the gospel and the quiet joy of sharing it with others.

You do not need to be extraordinary to be used by God.
You need to be available.

The same Spirit who stirred your heart to believe is still at work in the hearts of others. He is preparing conversations you have not yet had. He is drawing people you have not yet met.

This book is an invitation—not to mastery, but to participation. An invitation to carry the story that carried you. An invitation to trust that clarity is not weakness, but kindness—a gift to the person listening. An invitation to step into conversations with humility, courage, and hope.

The gospel does not need to be made powerful. It is powerful. It simply needs to be remembered—and shared.

Let's begin.

PART I

THE STORY BEHIND THE TOOL

WHEN THE GOSPEL
FIRST FOUND ME

I did not grow up in a Christian household. My family
practiced tribal spiritual traditions common in Tanzania—
rituals, sacrifices, and seeking guidance from ancestral spirits.
My father had two wives, and my mother was the second.
Through their marriage, they had three sons: Joshua, the oldest;
me, the middle; and Boaz, the youngest.

This was the spiritual environment that shaped my earliest
years—a world defined by divided loyalties, cultural tension,
and deep spiritual confusion. Our home lived under competing
spiritual influences: reverence for ancestral traditions, fear
of unseen forces, and a constant effort to maintain harmony
through rituals meant to protect us. There was no clear
undstanding of who God was—only a quiet awareness that the
spiritual world was powerful and unpredictable.

Everything changed the day someone shared the gospel with
my mother. She heard the message of Jesus, believed it, and
surrendered her life to Him. Her faith was genuine, and it
came at a cost. She prayed. She studied the Scriptures. She
longed to follow Jesus faithfully.

Looking back now, I can see that long before I ever reached for
God, He was already reaching for our family through her. As
her faith grew, she realized an unavoidable truth: she could no
longer remain my father's second wife. Following Jesus meant

stepping away from a marriage structure that did not honor God. And when she obeyed, everything in our home changed.

In many African societies—particularly where polygamy is common—a wife's departure is not seen as a private family matter; it is considered a public disgrace. My father's pride was bruised. His authority felt threatened. His reputation took a hit. The man who had once been warm and playful became cold and distant almost overnight. Anger, resentment, and shame consumed him.

In an attempt to punish her decision—and reclaim control—he turned that anger toward the people she loved most: her sons. He pulled Joshua and me out of school. He refused to provide for us. And eventually, he kicked us out of the house.

I was almost twelve years old.

In a single moment, we lost our home, our safety, and our sense of belonging. We became street children overnight— sleeping wherever we could and doing whatever it took to survive.

Life on the streets was not an adventure. It was humiliating, dangerous, and dehumanizing. Hunger became normal. Fear became familiar. Drugs dulled the pain. Theft became a matter of survival. Nights were cold, and days offered no promise of a better future. Gradually, my sense of self-worth began to erode, as though each day peeled away another layer of who I was.

By early 2002, the darkness inside me had become unbearable. One cold January night, I reached a breaking point and became convinced that ending my life was the only escape. But in a way I still cannot fully explain, God intervened. His mercy found me long before I ever thought to look for Him.

Not long after, I was reunited with my mother—the woman whose faith had already cost her nearly everything. Life with her was not a rescue into comfort. She was extremely poor. We slept in a small shack with a dirt floor. When it rained, there was often nowhere dry to lie down because the shack had no windows and little protection from the storm. There were countless days when we had no food at all.

And yet, in that place of deep lack, my mother's faith was unwavering. One practice in particular confused me. Even when we had nothing to eat, she would set the table. She would call us together, ask us to hold hands, and pray— believing that God would provide. I could not understand it. When you have gone a day or two without food, prayer can feel hollow. Setting a table with nothing on it felt almost cruel. But she was not pretending. She truly believed her God would provide.

One day, after we had followed that same routine—setting the table, holding hands, praying—and had just finished saying Amen, there was a knock at the door. A woman we did not know stood there holding a basket of food. She told us she had been praying and that the Holy Spirit had prompted her to bring food to our house.

I was stunned. That moment did not solve our poverty, but it disrupted my certainty. Something shifted inside me. Maybe there was something to my mother's faith. Maybe this Jesus she trusted was real. Maybe God truly saw us.

From that point on, my heart began to soften. I became open—slowly, cautiously—to learning about her faith. She connected me with her pastor, who patiently explained the gospel to me in ways I could understand. It did not happen overnight, but day by day, conversation by conversation, I sensed my heart being drawn closer to God.

Then came June 30, 2002—the day everything changed. At fourteen years old, after a season marked by abandonment, addiction, and deep hopelessness, I surrendered my life to Jesus Christ. In that moment, He saved me, restored me, and made me new.

"If anyone is in Christ, he is a new creation; the old has passed away; behold, the new has come" (2 Corinthians 5:17).

That promise became my story.

From the moment Jesus saved me, a fire ignited inside me—a burning desire to tell others what He had done. I had no formal theological training. I barely knew Scripture. My mother and I shared one Bible because we couldn't afford two. But I had a testimony, and that was enough.

Wherever I went, I would greet people and ask, "Can I tell you what Jesus has done in my life?" Then I shared the gospel as simply as I knew how: "I was broken and hopeless. Jesus saved me. And now I just want to tell people about His goodness."

It was simple.
Honest.
Unpolished.
True.

People listened—not because I was eloquent, but because the message was embodied. They could see the difference Christ had made in my life.

Some began calling me "Pastor Yusuph." Others would spot me from a distance and smile, already knowing exactly what I was about to say. Yet they still stayed and listened, because truth spoken simply has a way of reaching the heart.

It was during those early days—barefoot, newly redeemed, Bible in hand—that I learned something I now believe with my whole heart:

The gospel does not need complexity to carry power. It needs clarity. Clarity does not weaken the gospel—it reveals it.

Humble, honest simplicity can carry the full weight of God's truth. And yet, somewhere along the way, many of us began to treat the gospel as though it were fragile—something that required polish, precision, and perfect delivery. Not because it is complicated, but because we fear saying too little, explaining it imperfectly, or leaving questions unanswered.

So instead of trusting the power of the story, we try to master every detail—and in doing so, many grow hesitant to speak at all. We worry about saying the wrong thing. We fear not knowing enough Scripture. We feel pressure to be polished, articulate, and theologically airtight. And so instead of speaking, many remain silent—not from indifference, but from fear. But the truth remains. Simplicity is not the enemy of truth.

Jesus understood this. He spoke of seeds and soil, lamps and fields, bread and coins, fish and nets. He used what people already understood to reveal a Kingdom they did not yet know. He clarified the message instead of complicating it—trusting simple words to carry eternal truth. If Jesus entrusted the gospel to clarity rather than complexity, perhaps we can too.

Simplicity crosses cultures. It reaches children and elders alike. It comforts the anxious, strengthens the new believer, emboldens the quiet believer, and equips the whole Church for faithful witness. Simplicity is not a reduction of truth but a faithful expression of it—clarity that reveals, compassion that invites, humility that listens, and power that carries the gospel farther than complexity ever could.

In a world flooded with overwhelming information and noise, clarity becomes a gift. When God stirred the six lines in me, He was not giving me something complicated. He was calling me back to the gospel that saved me as a fourteen-year-old boy on the streets of Tanzania—a gospel simple enough to be drawn with a pen and powerful enough to change a life.

God created us.
We went astray.
Jesus came.
He saved us.

And when we put our faith in Him—when we trust what Jesus has done rather than what we can do—everything changes.

We are restored to God.
We become worshipers.
We go and tell.
That is the story.

And that is the heart behind this tool—a simple way for anyone, anywhere, to share the gospel with confidence and clarity.

THE HEART BEHIND THE SIX LINES CONCEPT

The gospel is many things—beautiful, eternal, and powerful—but at its core, it is a story. Not one story among many, but the true story of God and humanity—the story that gives meaning to every other story we tell. A story with a clear beginning, a clear rescue, and a clear purpose. A story every person is already living inside of, whether they realize it or not. And this story does not begin with humanity searching for God; it begins with God pursuing us.

Across generations and cultures, human beings are shaped by stories. Stories help us interpret the world, make sense of suffering, understand our longings, and locate meaning in the midst of pain. Every culture tells a story to explain who we are, why we are here, and what ultimately matters.

God, in His wisdom, gave us the gospel in story form for that very reason. The human heart receives story in a way it does not always receive propositions or arguments. The gospel is truth—unchanging and authoritative—but it is also a living narrative: relational, redemptive, and deeply personal. It does not merely inform us; it invites us in.

And yet, for many believers, sharing this story feels overwhelming. We worry we will say too much or too little. We fear misrepresenting God. We feel the pressure to have answers before we speak. And often, instead of stepping into the conversation, we stay silent—not because we lack conviction, but because we feel unprepared. This is where a simple conviction gave birth to the six lines:

The gospel should be easy to share.

Not watered down. Not trivialized. Not reduced. Simply made clear. Clarity does not come from mastering every nuance of theology. Clarity comes from remembering the story—and trusting it.

That is what this concept is meant to serve—not as a script to memorize, but as a way to hold the gospel with confidence, humility, and compassion.

Six lines.
Three movements.
One story.
One Savior.

Together, they guide us through the heart of the gospel in three movements that mirror the entire arc of Scripture:

Brokenness → Redemption → Worship.

And line by line, the story unfolds. The first two lines reveal the
condition we are born into—our separation from God and the
brokenness woven into every part of human life. The next two
lines reveal God's rescue—His love expressed through the cross,
and the salvation offered through Jesus Christ. The final two
lines reveal our new purpose—loving God and loving others in
response to His grace.

Before we draw the first line, there's an essential truth to
acknowledge: brokenness is not the beginning of the human
story. God created the world good (Genesis 1:31). Beauty existed
before fracture. Harmony came before conflict. Belonging
preceded shame.

But brokenness is the world each person is born into, and the
world everyone can recognize. Every heart feels it. Every culture
names it differently, yet every life eventually reaches the same
realization: something around us is not as it should be—and we
are not as we should be.

Brokenness may not be the first chapter of Scripture, but it
often serves as the doorway through which the gospel becomes
personal. It is where the ache of humanity meets the love of
God. And this is why anyone can share the gospel.

You don't need to be a pastor, a missionary, or a theologian.
You simply need to remember the story. The six lines are not
meant to be a technique to master. They are a simple, portable
way to carry the gospel with you—so you can share it with
confidence, compassion, and clarity.

Before we move on, let this settle into your heart: The six lines
aren't a step-by-step method for mastery; they are a story
worth remembering.

Now, with that foundation in place, we begin with the first two strokes of the pen—the lines that reveal the world we all find ourselves in: brokenness.

And with those lines, the story begins.

PART II

THE SIX LINES:
THE GOSPEL IN A STORY

THE FIRST TWO LINES: BROKENNESS

If you're drawing along, the first two strokes are simple: one diagonal line, then another crossing it.

Together, they form an X—a symbol recognized almost everywhere in the world as a sign that something is wrong, broken, or not as it was meant to be.

Before we can understand the beauty of the gospel, we must confront the reality of brokenness—not only around us, but also within us.

BROKENNESS IS THE STORY EVERY PERSON KNOWS

Brokenness appears in different ways across cultures, families, and individual lives, yet every person recognizes it. Some encounter it through sickness: diagnoses that disrupt life, bodies that fail, long nights in hospital corridors where hope feels thin. Others experience it through relationships—a marriage falling apart, a father

leaving, a mother withdrawing, a friendship ending without
warning.

Brokenness can also settle in the mind. Anxiety tightens
the chest. Depression drains desire. Shame lingers even in
moments that should feel bright. It shows up through loss: a
loved one gone too soon, a dream collapsing, a future slipping
away. It appears through injustice as well—poverty that
erodes dignity, systems that wound, violence that scars entire
communities. And sometimes brokenness is quieter still—a
persistent ache of not belonging, the feeling of being unseen,
or inner emptiness that no amount of success, love, or striving
can fill.

Whether we live in Tanzania, America, or somewhere in
between, the human heart eventually reaches the same
conclusion.

Something is terribly broken.

Scripture puts it plainly: "For all have sinned and fall short of
the glory of God" (Romans 3:23, ESV). Brokenness is not only
what happens to us; it is also what lives in us—sin, fear, pride,
selfishness, rebellion.

We fall short of reflecting God's goodness and living in the
relationship we were created for. Every person carries some
expression of this fracture. And I know this reality intimately.

MY STORY OF THE X

You may remember from the previous chapter that a cold night in January 2002 brought me to the edge of ending my life. But that moment had a long story behind it—one shaped by abandonment, fear, and a childhood that unraveled too quickly.

Life on the streets was cruel. Hunger was constant. But what cut the deepest was knowing there was food in my father's house while I slept outside, unwanted and alone.

Before any of this, my father had been a fun and caring dad—Baba, as we say in Swahili. He wasn't perfect, but he was present. He provided in the ways he understood. He protected. Our home had been a place of warmth and familiarity.

But when my mother left the polygamous marriage to follow Jesus, something inside him changed. It wasn't demonic possession—it was what happens when wounded honor, cultural shame, spiritual darkness, and unprocessed pain collide in the human heart. A shadow overtook him. The Baba we knew slowly disappeared. His eyes hardened. His words sharpened. Home shifted from a place of belonging into a place of tension and fear.

And eventually that bitterness and spiritual darkness turned directly toward my older brother Joshua and me.

One day, he kicked us out of the house, and from that moment forward, we were street children—boys with nowhere to belong.

Hunger wore us down. Nights grew colder. Hope thinned. In desperation, I would sometimes sneak back into the house for food—tiptoeing, praying I would not be seen.

Then one afternoon, everything changed. I slipped inside, grabbed something to eat, and suddenly heard the door slam shut behind me.

My father stood in the doorway with a look that froze my entire body with fear. He grabbed me, tore away my clothes, bound my hands and feet like someone restraining an animal, and beat me with a cane again and again. It was a rage no child should ever face and a brutality no father should ever unleash.

My voice gave out.
My body shook uncontrollably.
My heart fractured under the weight of betrayal.
One question echoed inside me long after the bruises faded:

"How can a father do this to his own child?"

When he finally untied me, he looked at his bruised, trembling son and said words that cut deeper than any wound, "Leave my house. If I ever see you again, I will kill you."

To anyone who has experienced violence or abuse, hear this clearly: what happened to me was evil. It was not my fault. It did not reflect the heart of God. Though He permitted it within His sovereignty, He did not approve of it, delight in it, or turn away from me in it—even if I could not yet see His nearness.

I walked away that day feeling discarded, unseen, and utterly worthless. In my young mind, rejection felt final. That night, I became convinced my life no longer had meaning.

WHAT BROKENNESS REALLY MEANS

My story is just one expression of brokenness, but everyone carries their own wounds.

Brokenness isn't just a concept; it's a real experience. It's the collapse of what we trusted, the wound that refuses to heal, the shame that whispers lies, and the painful distance between what God intended and what we now face.

Scripture clearly shows that brokenness results from sin—the kind we inherit, the kind we suffer, and the kind we commit. It is the world as it is, not the world as God originally made it.

WHERE THIS STORY TRULY BEGINS

Brokenness didn't come out of nowhere. It has a beginning— and that beginning isn't pain, but goodness.

Before sin, shame, or fear existed, God created the world whole, harmonious, and beautiful. Humanity was made in His image—to reflect His character, live in unbroken relationship

with Him, and fill the world with His goodness (Genesis
1:26–28).

"And God saw everything that he had made, and behold, it was
very good." (Genesis 1:31, ESV)

But in Genesis 3, Adam and Eve chose to distrust God's
goodness and step outside His loving rule. Everything changed.
Sin entered the story. Death followed. Fear, shame, fractured
relationships, and spiritual separation wove themselves into
the human experience.

Scripture says, "...sin came into the world through one man,
and death through sin..." (Romans 5:12, ESV), and "...your
iniquities have made a separation between you and your
God..." (Isaiah 59:2, ESV). Since that moment, brokenness has
marked every generation. We inherit it. We feel it. And we
contribute to it.

BEYOND PRESENT PAIN: THE DEEPER REALITY OF SPIRITUAL DEATH

Our emotional and physical pain is devastating, but Scripture
reveals an even deeper reality:

Sin brings spiritual death.

Paul writes, "And you were dead in the trespasses and sins in
which you once walked..." (Ephesians 2:1, ESV).

Dead—not merely wounded, discouraged, or lost.

Dead—unable to return to God on our own.

Dead—unable to revive ourselves spiritually.

And unless Someone intervenes, that spiritual death becomes eternal separation from the God who created us. Brokenness in this life is heavy, but eternal separation from God is the heaviest weight of all. This is the full weight of the X.

BROKENNESS ISN'T THE BEGINNING — AND IT ISN'T THE END

Although brokenness characterizes much of our human experience, it is neither the first nor the last chapter. Our longing for peace, belonging, wholeness, justice, and connection is not accidental; it is memory. Our souls remember Eden. Brokenness hurts precisely because it violates what we were created for.

For many of us, brokenness becomes the doorway through which we begin to recognize our need for God. It awakens questions we cannot ignore:

Why is the world like this?
Why do I hurt?
Is there hope?
Is there Someone who can restore what is broken?

The X reveals the truth: We are broken people in a broken world, spiritually dead and unable to save ourselves. If the story ended here, the gospel would only be devastating.

But it does not end here.

Into this ache—into the wounds we carry, the questions we cannot answer, and the spiritual death we cannot escape—God moves toward us. He pursues, loves, and rescues us.

In the next chapter, we draw lines 3 and 4—the lines that reveal God's answer to our brokenness.

And those lines change everything.

THE NEXT TWO LINES: REDEMPTION

If you're drawing along, the next two strokes are simple. Start by drawing a long vertical line, then place a horizontal stroke slightly above the center.

With just these two lines, a familiar and globally recognized shape emerges—the cross. In nearly every culture on earth, the cross stands as a symbol of hope, sacrifice, and rescue: two ordinary lines, but an extraordinary message. Before we can understand our response to this rescue, we must pause and look closely at the cross—the beauty, the weight, the meaning, and the redemption it offers.

OUR GREAT NEED

Redemption only makes sense when we understand the problem it addresses. The cross is not an accessory of Christianity; it is a necessity (1 Corinthians 1:18). To grasp its power, we must see our need through the lens of God's holiness.

Scripture describes God as holy—utterly pure, morally perfect, and set apart. The angels cry, "Holy, holy, holy is the LORD of hosts" (Isaiah 6:3). His holiness means He cannot ignore sin or coexist with evil. Humanity, created to live in His presence, lost that privilege through rebellion.

God's justice flows from His holiness. If God ignored evil, He would cease to be good. Sin carries guilt, consequence, and a moral debt. Paul writes, "For the wages of sin is death..." (Romans 6:23). This death is not only physical; it includes spiritual separation from God that began in the garden and continues in every human heart.

Scripture says we are "dead in our trespasses and sins" (Ephesians 2:1). To be spiritually dead is to be cut off from the life of God—unable to revive ourselves, unable to erase guilt, unable to return to Him.

We need rescue—divine, decisive, undeserved rescue.

Humanity's dilemma is this:

God is holy and just.
We are sinful and guilty.
We are separated from Him and powerless to fix ourselves.

If reconciliation is to happen, it must be God who takes the first step. And He did.

GOD'S GREAT GIFT

Into our helplessness, God moved with love and purpose.

The cross is not humanity climbing toward heaven—it is
heaven descending toward humanity.

Jesus Christ—fully God and fully man—entered our world,
lived the life we failed to live, and willingly gave Himself as
our substitute. He stood where we should have stood. He
carried what we could not carry. He bore what we could not
bear. Peter writes, "He himself bore our sins in his body on the
tree" (1 Peter 2:24).

And then Paul gives us one of the most breathtaking
summaries of the gospel: "For our sake he made him to be
sin who knew no sin,so that in Him we might become the
righteousness of God" (2 Corinthians 5:21, ESV).

This one verse unveils the Great Exchange:

the innocent One becomes sin,
the guilty one becomes righteous;

the spotless One takes our stain,
the condemned stand forgiven and restored.

Our sin was placed on Him.
His righteousness is placed on us.

Our debt transferred to Him.
His life given to us.

The wrath of God is not unpredictable rage. It is His holy and
steady opposition to sin—His refusal to allow evil to triumph.
On the cross, Jesus willingly absorbed this righteous judgment
in our place. Isaiah foretold this moment: "He was pierced
for our transgressions; he was crushed for our iniquities... and
with his wounds we are healed" (Isaiah 53:5).

On the cross, Jesus fulfilled the entire Old Testament
sacrificial system. John the Baptist called Him "the Lamb of
God, who takes away the sin of the world" (John 1:29). He
became the final, perfect, sufficient sacrifice. When Jesus
declared, "It is finished" (John 19:30), He announced the
completion of a work humanity could never accomplish.

The resurrection confirmed the Father's acceptance of His
sacrifice. Through Jesus' resurrection, sin is defeated, death is
conquered, and Satan is disarmed (Colossians 2:15). The empty
tomb stands as God's eternal declaration that redemption is
real, complete, and available—freedom purchased, debt paid,
and broken lives restored.

Redemption is not merely an idea—it is power.

WHEN REDEMPTION BECAME PERSONAL FOR ME

This theology is not just an idea in my mind; it's a story God
has woven into my personal history. When Jesus saved me at

fourteen, something within me immediately awakened—a deep desire to share what He had done.

By sixteen, I knew I wanted to dedicate my life to proclaiming His love. I traveled from village to village across Tanzania, preaching the gospel. Some places welcomed the message; others rejected it. Some greeted us with joy; others threw stones.

At eighteen, I traveled to Ujiji, a town known for its hostility toward the gospel. While sharing Christ there, I was arrested and thrown into prison.

For days, I wrestled with confusion. Why would God allow this? Why would He interrupt the work He had called me to do?

In that dim, cold cell, the Holy Spirit spoke gently to my heart: "Yusuph, I have brought you here so I can set you free." At first, it made no sense.

How can you speak of freedom in a locked cell?

Then I sensed the Spirit continue: "You preach forgiveness, but you have not forgiven your father." Those words pierced deeper than any prison walls ever could. I resisted them. I told God I could never forgive the man who had beaten me, abandoned me, and cast me into the streets.

But God reminded me that my own sin had nailed His Son to the cross—and still He forgave me freely, fully, without hesitation. Scripture says, "God shows his love for us in that while we were still sinners, Christ died for us" (Romans 5:8, ESV). In that moment, the truth of the cross became deeply personal.

I fell to my knees and wept—broken not by my father's sin this time, but by my own. I asked Jesus to forgive the unforgiveness in my heart and to help me forgive my father as He had forgiven me.

Though I was still behind prison bars, something shifted inside me. I was no longer confined in the same way. The bitterness that had held me captive began to loosen its grip. For the first time, I felt free. That freedom did not stay hidden.

Day after day, I told the other prisoners about the cross—about mercy, about a Savior who forgives completely. What began as quiet conversations grew into something only God could orchestrate. By His grace, nearly thirty men surrendered their lives to Christ while we were there together. In a place meant to confine and silence, the gospel moved freely.

Three months later, I was released from prison. When I walked out of those gates, I carried more than physical freedom—I carried a softened heart. I reached out to my father, and slowly we began rebuilding what had been shattered.

It was not quick or easy; redemption rarely is. Trust had to be relearned. Conversations were careful. Healing came in small, fragile steps. But even in those fragile steps, God was quietly at work in both of us, doing something neither of us could have imagined.

Five years later, when I was twenty-three, in August 2011, I had the sacred privilege of leading my Baba—my daddy—to Christ. And the miracle is not simply that I forgave him. The miracle is not even that he prayed with me. The miracle is that God saved us both.

I watched him weep.
I watched him repent.
I watched him receive the same grace that had rescued me
years earlier.

In that moment, Genesis 50:20 came alive: "what the enemy
intended for evil, God used for good." This is redemption—not
a doctrine alone, but a miracle that transforms real stories, real
wounds, and real people.

OUR GREAT RESPONSE

Redemption invites a response—not one of striving, but of
faith and surrender. The cross calls us to come as we are—
broken, guilty, weary, ashamed—and receive the life only Jesus
can give. Scripture describes this response in movements
simple enough for a child, yet deep enough to shape a lifetime:

REPENT — turning away from sin and toward God (Acts 3:19;
Luke 24:47). Repentance is not self-improvement; it is honest
agreement with God about our sin and a turning of the heart
toward His mercy.

BELIEVE — trusting that Jesus' life, death, and resurrection
are enough to save us (John 3:16; Romans 10:9). Belief is not
blind; it confidently rests in His finished work.

RECEIVE — embracing forgiveness, freedom, and new life as
God's gift (John 1:12). Salvation is not a wage to earn but a gift
to accept.

SURRENDER — yielding our lives to His leadership and love (Mark 8:34; Romans 12:1). Surrender is the joyful act of giving our lives to the One who sacrificed everything for us.

Perhaps as you read this chapter, something is stirring in your heart—a longing for forgiveness, a desire for freedom, an awareness that Jesus is calling your name.

If that is you, hear this clearly:

Jesus can save you—just as He saved me. If He reached a broken teenager living on the streets of Tanzania, He can reach you. If He met me in a prison cell and set my heart free, He can meet you anywhere. If He redeemed my story and restored what felt impossible, He can redeem yours.

Salvation is not earned. It is received.

And Scripture promises: "Everyone who calls on the name of the Lord will be saved" (Romans 10:13). If you want to receive Jesus today, you can call out to Him right now—even silently. God hears the honest cry of a humble heart.

No specific words can save you. A prayer does not rescue you— Jesus does. What matters is not a formula, but faith: turning from your sin and placing your trust in Him.

You might express that trust in a prayer like this:

"Jesus, I know I am a sinner, and I cannot save myself. Thank You for dying for my sin and rising again. I believe You are the only One who can forgive me and make me new. I turn from my sin and place my

trust in You. Please save me, forgive me, and lead me from this day forward. Amen."

If you have sincerely turned to Jesus and trusted Him—even if your words were different—then according to God's Word, you belong to Him. You have been forgiven, rescued, and adopted into God's family (John 10:28; Romans 8:38–39).

Redemption is the heart of the gospel.
It is the center of the story.
It is the power of God for everyone who believes.

And now, as redeemed people, we learn how to live. The final two lines reveal what this redeemed life looks like—how we walk with God, how we love Him, and how we love others in response to His grace.

THE FINAL TWO LINES: WORSHIP
(LOVING GOD + LOVING OTHERS)

If you're drawing along, the final two lines are simple. Draw one line pointing upward. Draw another extending outward.

These two strokes reveal the natural response of a heart transformed by the gospel. They show what happens after redemption—how God begins reshaping us the moment we believe. Together, they point to a life oriented in two directions: upward toward God and outward toward the people He loves.

Jesus summarized this when He declared that the greatest commandments are to "Love the Lord your God with all your heart and with all your soul and with all your mind" and to "love your neighbor as yourself" (Matthew 22:37–39).

The upward life and the outward life. The worshiping life and the serving life. A redeemed heart responding to a redeeming God.

Worship is much more than singing on Sunday; it is the daily posture of a believer—living with gratitude, obedience, and reliance on the God who saved us.

Redemption is not the end of our story; it marks the beginning of a new one. These final two lines illustrate what that new life looks like.

THE UPWARD LIFE — LOVING GOD

The first line points upward because the redeemed life begins with God Himself.

Through Jesus, we are forgiven, restored, and adopted into His family. Loving God is not a duty to perform; it is a relationship to enjoy—a response to grace and a movement of the heart toward the One who moved toward us first (1 John 4:19).

Scripture gives us rhythms—gracious patterns that shape our love for God over time. They are not rigid formulas but steady invitations that anchor our lives in Him.

We love God through His Word, not as an obligation but as nourishment: "Man shall not live by bread alone, but by every word that comes from the mouth of God" (Matthew 4:4).

We love Him through honest prayer—words that are real, not polished—trusting that He listens and responds: "The Lord is near to all who call on him, to all who call on him in truth" (Psalm 145:18).

We love Him through obedience, not to earn His approval but because we trust His wisdom: "If you love me, you will keep my commandments" (John 14:15).

We love Him through community, sharing life with His people in worship, encouragement, and accountability:

"They devoted themselves to the apostles' teaching and the fellowship, to the breaking of bread and the prayers" (Acts 2:42).

We love Him through dependence—seeking the Spirit's help in our weakness and trusting His power to sustain what we cannot carry on our own: "Apart from me you can do nothing" (John 15:5).

And upward love often shows itself in quiet, hidden moments:

a whispered surrender before a difficult decision,
a confession of sin,
a moment of gratitude in a busy day,
a step of obedience no one else sees.

The upward life is not about perfection—
it is about direction.

Day by day, redeemed people turn their hearts toward the God who loved them first.

The second line extends outward because the love God pours into us was never meant to stop with us. Jesus never separated loving God from loving others; the two are inseparable.

Love for God overflows into love for people, and love for people reflects a heart transformed by God. When grace reshapes us, it inevitably reshapes how we care for the world around us.

Sometimes outward love means sharing the gospel. Paul says we are "ambassadors for Christ" (2 Corinthians 5:20). This does not require eloquence—only willingness. It may look like explaining what Jesus has done in your life, offering prayer to someone in pain, or drawing the six lines for a friend searching for hope.

Other times, outward love becomes compassion in action. "Let us not love in word or talk but in deed and in truth" (1 John 3:18). Real love takes shape in visible ways: comforting the grieving, feeding the hungry, helping a struggling family, forgiving someone who wounded us, or standing beside those the world overlooks.

Outward love varies from season to season. For one believer, it may mean mentoring a child or encouraging a coworker. For another, it may look like visiting hospitals, supporting a neighbor through loss, or quietly meeting practical needs. In every case, outward love begins with availability: "Lord, use me to show Your love wherever You send me."

WORSHIP AS A LIFESTYLE — A LIFE OF SURRENDER

When upward love for God and outward love for others come together, worship becomes more than a moment. It becomes a way of life—a posture of surrender, gratitude, and obedience.

Paul captures it beautifully: "Present your bodies as a living sacrifice, holy and acceptable to God, which is your spiritual worship" (Romans 12:1). Worship is offering our entire selves to God—our gifts, our wounds, our future, our story.

And sometimes, the deepest worship flows from places of pain.

I learned this in my own story. From the moment Jesus saved me, I sought to walk in obedience—imperfectly but sincerely. Over the years, I have seen how God has shaped my life in ways I never expected. One of those ways came through the deepest sorrow I have ever known.

You already know about my brother Joshua and me. But our youngest brother, Boaz, is woven into my story as well, and his life shaped my calling in ways I could not have foreseen.

Boaz was still young when chaos fractured our family. For a time, his age shielded him from the full force of what Joshua and I endured. But that protection did not last. When my father discovered that Joshua and I had reunited with our mother, he made another devastating decision—he abandoned Boaz too.

One afternoon in the fall of 2002, Joshua and I returned home to find our little brother sitting quietly on the doorstep. He was twelve years old. No warning. No explanation. Just a boy left behind.

We had almost nothing to offer him. We were still rebuilding our own lives, still learning how to survive, still piecing together hope from what had been shattered. But that day, we made a promise: whatever it took, we would give him a chance at a different future.

We worked long days—twelve to fourteen hours—earning about $1.50 each, saving everything we could. Boaz stayed in school. He carried himself with a quiet determination that humbled me. He refused to let his circumstances define him. Step by step, year by year, he moved forward.

In 2016, he graduated from university—the first in our family to do so. The following year, we stood beside him and celebrated his wedding with deep joy and gratitude.

Then came September 2017.

I was living in the United States when word reached me that Boaz had fallen ill and been admitted to a hospital in Mwanza. I called him right away. His voice was weak but calm. We spoke briefly. I told him I loved him and promised to call again soon.

I had no idea those would be our last words.

Not long after, Joshua called with the news. My mind heard him, but my heart refused to believe it. Numbness took over—

sharp, disorienting, surreal. I booked the earliest flight I could, but the long hours in the air felt like floating between two worlds: one where Boaz still lived, and one where he no longer did.

Three days after that call, I stood beside Boaz's coffin—stunned, hurting, overwhelmed by a kind of pain I had never felt before.

We had prayed for his future. We had worked to give him a different life. We had sacrificed to protect his opportunities. We had hoped he would live out the story God was writing in him. And still, his story on earth ended far sooner than we dreamed.

In that valley of grief, God met me—not with explanations, but with His presence; not with answers, but with Himself.

As I wrestled, a quiet conviction began to take shape: God does not waste pain. In His mysterious wisdom, He weaves purpose into what we would never choose. As I surrendered my grief to Him, I sensed Him speaking—not audibly, but unmistakably:

"Go. You are ready now."

It was not a call to forget my brother or move on. It was an invitation to trust Him—to believe He could redeem even this.

Obedience didn't begin with a strategy. It began with surrender. And that surrender slowly grew into what would eventually become Twelve21 Global—a ministry built on obedience, compassion, and worship. It began with a simple yes to follow, trust, and walk with God on an unknown path.

Over time, God opened doors in communities familiar with the same kind of brokenness I once experienced. What started as one redeemed life grew into a community committed to living out the gospel both in word and action.

But hear this clearly: This is not primarily a story about an organization.

This is about what God can do through a surrendered life.

This is worship—the life of surrender. Worship is trusting God when we don't understand. Worship is loving Him and loving others through joy and tears. Worship is believing that God is present, wise, and good even when the path isn't clear.

God does not waste our pain.

He redeems it and uses surrendered hearts to carry His hope into the world. Your story may look different from mine. Your calling may unfold quietly or dramatically. But if you belong to Jesus, this much is certain: you are not here by accident.

God has left you here on purpose and for a purpose. Worship, then, is your response—a life turned upward toward Him and outward toward the world He loves.

Now that all six lines are drawn, we're ready for the next step: learning how to share this simple picture with someone who needs to hear the greatest story ever told.

HOW TO USE
THE SIX LINES

HOW TO SHARE
THE SIX LINES

One of the most beautiful aspects of the six lines concept is its simplicity.

You don't need formal training, a memorized script, or a particular personality.

All you need is something to write with, something to write on, and a heart willing to join God in what He is already doing.

Whether you're in a remote Tanzanian village, a school cafeteria, a workplace break room, a bus stop, or your own living room, this simple picture can open the door to a natural, Spirit-led conversation about the hope we have in Christ.

Here is how you can share it with confidence, clarity, and compassion.

STEP 1: BROKENNES - Draw the X (lines 1 & 2)

Begin by drawing two diagonal lines that form an X.

Then you might say:

"This X represents our world. It's beautiful, but it's also broken. And that brokenness isn't just around us—it's inside us too."

You don't need a long explanation. You don't need statistics or philosophy. Brokenness is universal because everyone carries some part of it. You can connect brokenness to whatever fits the moment—broken relationships, fear or anxiety, shame or guilt, injustice, depression, trauma, sickness, loss, or the quiet ache people feel when life is not what it should be.

Scripture teaches that brokenness ultimately comes from sin—humanity turning away from God's good design (Genesis 3; Romans 5:12).

Your role here is not to impress someone. Your role is to help them name a reality they already feel: something is wrong in the world, and something is wrong in us.

STEP 2: REDEMPTION - Draw the Cross (lines 3 & 4)

Next, draw one vertical line and one horizontal line—forming the cross. Then say:

"God sees our brokenness, but He didn't leave us there. Jesus came, lived the life we could not live, and died the death our sin deserved. Through the cross, God offers forgiveness, healing, and a restored relationship with Him."

This is the heart of the gospel: Jesus steps into our brokenness to rescue us. And this is where the invitation naturally belongs.

Before moving on, take a moment to slow down. Look the person in the eyes. Let silence work. Then gently ask:

"This is where God invites us to respond—to turn from sin and trust in Jesus. The Bible says that anyone who believes in Him will be forgiven and made new. Would you like to take that step today?"

No pressure. No manipulation. Just an open door.

If they are not ready, you stay with them. If they have questions, you welcome them. If they want to receive Christ, you guide them in a simple prayer—asking Jesus to forgive their sin and give them new life.

Only after creating intentional space for their response—whatever it may be—do you move on.

STEP 3: WORSHIP - Draw the Final Two Lines (lines 5&6)

Now draw one line pointing upward and one extending outward. Then say:

"When we receive God's forgiveness through Jesus, He gives us a new direction. He turns our hearts upward to love Him and outward to love others."

These lines show what the redeemed life looks like. The Christian life is not about instant perfection—it is about Spirit-led transformation.

You can explain briefly what this looks like: learning to know God through Scripture, talking to Him in prayer, walking with

His people, growing in obedience,living with compassion,
and letting His love shape how we treat others.

This keeps the focus on worship—upward love for God and
outward love for people.

HOW TO SHARE AS YOU DRAW

As you sketch the six lines, here is a simple way to
summarize:

Brokenness: Life is broken because of sin in the world and
in us.

Redemption (with invitation): Jesus came to rescue us.
God invites us to turn from sin and trust Him.

Worship: When we trust Jesus, He gives us a new way to
live—loving God and loving others.

That's it—clear truth, spoken in love, carried by the Spirit.

*Keep it simple. Remember: God does not ask you to be
eloquent. He asks you to be faithful.*

You don't need perfect words. You don't need every answer.
You don't need a polished explanation. If you can draw six
lines and share what they mean, you are ready.

Six lines.
Three symbols.
One story.
One Savior.

BEFORE MOVING ON

You truly can do this—and you do not do it alone. Jesus promised, "All authority in heaven and on earth has been given to me... and behold, I am with you always" (Matthew 28:18–20).

As you draw, trust that He is already at work in the person sitting across from you—preparing their heart, opening their eyes, and drawing them to Himself.

You are not creating something from nothing;
you are stepping into what God is already doing.

This tool is simple enough for a child to understand and clear enough for a new believer to share the very same day. God has always delighted in using ordinary people who simply say yes.

In the next chapter, we will explore how to recognize spiritual openness, begin meaningful conversations, and walk patiently with people as God leads them toward faith.'

RECOGNIZING GOSPEL MOMENTS

In 2017, I traveled to Maisome Island, a small fishing island on Lake Victoria in Tanzania. It is one of those places the world knows almost nothing about—remote, rugged, quietly beautiful, and deeply unreached.

I went with a small team to encourage and train the local church planters faithfully serving in that isolated community. As we walked through the village one morning, a local pastor said, "There's someone I want you to meet," and he led me toward a cluster of weather-beaten homes near the shore.

Fishermen repaired their nets in the morning light. Children played barefoot in the sand. The wind carried the scent of lake water and burning firewood. That's where I met Revocatus, a 56-year-old man known across the island as the "town drunk" and a womanizer.

His reputation followed him everywhere, but when I looked into his eyes, I saw something deeper—a soul carrying more weight than any human heart was created to bear.

We sat outside his home. After a quiet moment, I asked, "How have you been these days?" He shrugged, "I'm okay... just tired." But the heaviness behind his eyes told a different story.

So we continued talking—slowly, naturally—about life, work, regrets, and the burdens he carried. As he spoke, something in his heart loosened. His posture softened. His answers lengthened. His guard lowered—slowly, then noticeably—like someone unburdening himself without fully realizing it.

When the moment felt right, I shared why I had come to the island—how Jesus had met me in my own brokenness, healed me, forgiven me, and given me new purpose. I told him that the same Jesus loved him too.

He listened quietly, almost cautiously, as though afraid to believe hope could reach someone like him. Then, with fragile honesty, he whispered, "Yusuph... I don't think God could ever want someone like me."

That was the wound beneath all the other wounds—not whether God existed, but whether God could love him. I met his eyes and said, "You are not the sum of your past. God made you in His image. He knows everything you've done, and He still sent Jesus for you—not because of who you are, but because of who He is."

The words fell into him like rain on dry ground. His face trembled. Tears formed. And right there on that remote island, sitting in the dust outside his home, Revocatus surrendered his life to Jesus.

Then something remarkable happened. He stood, wiped his tears, and said, "My friends need to hear this." Within minutes, he was calling neighbors to come listen. The man many had dismissed as hopeless became the one pointing others to hope.

Moments like this remind me that the gospel is not merely a message to explain—it is a living story breathed by God, carried by ordinary people, and received in unexpected places.

There are "Revocatus moments" everywhere: in cities and villages, in noisy streets and quiet kitchens, on buses and fishing boats, in offices and farms, across every culture and generation.

Brokenness has many faces, but the ache it creates is universal. And the hope of Jesus is for all.

WHAT THIS STORY REVEALS ABOUT GOSPEL MOMENTS

The conversation with Revocatus reveals a pattern—five simple, Spirit-led movements that open the human heart to the gospel. These movements are not a formula; the Holy Spirit is never mechanical. But they help us recognize and join what God is already doing.

1. Recognize Spiritual Openness

Spiritual openness is typically quiet and subtle. Most people do not say, "Tell me about Jesus." Instead, openness shows up through exhaustion, regret, sadness, frustration, emptiness, restlessness, or grief. It appears in tired eyes, a slumped posture, a trembling voice, a sigh that slips out, or a confession spoken almost accidentally.

Across cultures, human hearts reveal themselves through small cracks, and those cracks are often where the Holy Spirit is already at work (John 6:44). With Revocatus, brokenness appeared in his eyes long before it did in his words.

And when we learn to notice those whispers, we step onto holy ground.

2. Ask Genuine, Compassionate Questions

Once openness is recognized, the next step is disarmingly simple: ask honest, compassionate questions. Not strategic questions designed to transition into a gospel presentation. Not rehearsed evangelism lines. Human questions. Dignifying questions. Questions that communicate, "I see you, and I care."

Questions like:

"How have you really been these days?"
"What has been weighing on you lately?"
"How is your heart doing?"

People open up where they feel safe. Compassionate questions create that safety. Jesus Himself used questions to draw people out of hiding—the woman at the well, the blind man, the disciples. Questions are bridges. With Revocatus, one simple question began to unlock years of hidden pain.

3. Share Your Story Honestly and Briefly

As trust grows, people naturally wonder why you care. This is where your story becomes a bridge—not a performance, not a polished testimony, but simple honesty about what Jesus has done in your life.

Your story makes the gospel believable. Vulnerability invites vulnerability. When someone hears how Jesus rescued you, it awakens the hope that He can rescue them, too. You do not need a dramatic story; you need a true one. A surrendered story. A story that makes grace feel possible.

When I shared with Revocatus how Jesus found me in my brokenness, forgave me, and gave me purpose, it opened his heart to believe that the same grace could reach him.

4. Sense the Right Moment to Share the Gospel

This is the movement many believers fear, but it is where the Holy Spirit most clearly helps us. The gospel is not a speech. It is an invitation—and invitations require timing. Often, the right moment reveals itself through statements like:

"I feel lost."
"I feel empty."
"I don't think God wants me."
"I don't know what to do anymore."

These are sacred windows. They are not moments to pressure someone; they are moments to offer hope. That's when you gently say, "Can I show you something simple that explains what Jesus has done for us?"

This is where the six lines tool becomes a gift—a visual doorway into God's story intersecting with theirs (Acts 8:29).

5. Surrender the Outcome to God

This final movement is the most freeing: we are not
responsible for the results. We cannot save anyone. We cannot
manufacture repentance or produce faith. That work belongs
to God alone.

Some respond immediately, like Revocatus. Some need months
or years. Some walk away but return later.

Our role is faithfulness; God's role is transformation. Paul
says, "I planted, Apollos watered, but God gave the growth"
(1 Corinthians 3:7). This frees us from pressure and pride. We
draw the lines. God draws the heart.

MOVING FORWARD

These five movements—recognizing openness, asking with
compassion, sharing honestly, sensing the Spirit's timing, and
surrendering the outcome—form the relational foundation for
every gospel conversation.

In the next chapter, we will explore how these movements
unfold in everyday life through real examples across different
cultures, settings, and personalities.

GOSPEL MOMENTS IN ORDINARY PLACES

A few years ago, I was traveling back home to Dallas after a trip to Kome Island—one of the remote islands on Lake Victoria in Tanzania. If you have ever made that journey, you know it drains you of everything. The trip begins with a ferry ride across the lake, followed by a three-hour bus ride on a potholed dirt road—what Tanzanians jokingly call the "local bus massage." Then another ferry, then a short regional flight, then two back-to-back eight-hour international flights, and finally a three-hour connection into Texas.

By the time you reach Dallas/Fort Worth International Airport, you're held together by prayer, determination, and the hope of your own bed. You don't want a conversation. You don't want eye contact. You don't even want to hear your name. You just want to go home.

On that particular day, I was exhausted—the kind of exhaustion that doesn't sit on the surface but sinks into your bones. As I approached U.S. Customs, I braced myself for the routine: passport, fingerprint, "Welcome home," and done.

But the officer glanced at my passport, looked up, and asked the one question I didn't feel ready for: "So... what were you doing in Tanzania?"

My spirit flickered with excitement, but my body resisted immediately. *Not now, Yusuph. Keep it simple. Say you were visiting family. Go home.*

I stood there caught between exhaustion and opportunity, between comfort and calling, between silence and obedience. Then a whisper rose in my heart:

"When will you ever stand in front of this man again?"

So instead of the easy answer, I told the truth. I told him about Kome Island—a place where the gospel is slowly breaking through layers of spiritual darkness. I told him about the villages we visited, the pastors we encouraged, and the moments where people heard the name of Jesus for the very first time. I shared how men and women on a remote fishing island opened their hearts to Christ with tears and relief.

He didn't interrupt.
He didn't rush.
He didn't check his watch.
He listened as if his soul were thirsty.

When I finished, he closed my passport slowly and said softly: "Mr. Emmanuel... you have encouraged me so much. I truly needed this today."

Behind me, a long line of tired travelers probably wondered why this African man was being held for so long. But if they only knew.

Right there, under fluorescent airport lights and immigration signs, God created holy ground. Not because I planned it. Not

because I had energy. Not because I was ready. But because
God was.

That is the heart of this chapter—not sermons, not stages,
not perfect timing, but ordinary moments that become
extraordinary when we are willing to say, "Yes, Lord."

GOSPEL CONVERSATIONS IN EVERYDAY LIFE

Gospel conversations don't always happen in perfect moments
or ideal conditions. Most often, they occur in the middle of
everyday life—while you're tired, distracted, or thinking about
something else. But the Holy Spirit does not wait for perfect
conditions. He prepares hearts long before you arrive and
arranges moments you could never predict.

The six lines serve these moments not because they are clever,
but because they are clear. They give shape to the story God is
already writing in someone's heart. They anchor conversations
that might otherwise drift away. These everyday moments
become sacred when our eyes are open and our hearts are
receptive.

WHEN YOU ONLY HAVE A MOMENT

Some opportunities are brief—standing in line, waiting for
a ride, settling into a plane seat, or speaking with a cashier.
Many believers assume these moments are too small to matter,
but Scripture tells a different story.

Philip had only a limited stretch of road with the Ethiopian
eunuch (Acts 8:26–39). Jesus had a brief exchange with
Zacchaeus beneath a tree (Luke 19:1–10). Time did not limit
what God intended to do.

Brief encounters can be powerful precisely because they are
simple. When time is limited, clarity matters more. You are
not delivering a lecture; you are planting a seed. A picture. A
sentence. A spark of hope. A thirty-second sketch of the six
lines may be the first clear glimpse of the gospel someone has
ever received.

What feels small to you may be sacred to God.

Even a fleeting moment, surrendered to Him, can echo into
eternity.

WHEN YOU'RE SITTING WITH SOMEONE WHO IS HURTING

Pain softens soil the way rain prepares hardened ground. Grief,
disappointment, relational conflict, fear, or confusion often

bring people to the edge of honesty. In these spaces, human hearts are strangely more open than we expect.

This is why James wrote, "Let every person be quick to hear" (James 1:19). Listening is not passive; it is spiritual work. A listening posture communicates dignity, safety, and compassion—three things wounded hearts rarely receive.

When someone is hurting, you don't rush to solutions or explanations. You sit with them in the ache. You mirror Jesus, who "was moved with compassion" (Matthew 9:36).

In these tender moments, the "X" gives language to what they already feel: "Life is broken." The cross points to the One who enters suffering, not avoids it. The final lines show that God doesn't just redeem—He restores. The gospel does not erase pain, but it reorients it. It whispers, "You are not alone, and this is not the end."

WHEN SOMEONE ASKS WHY YOUR FAITH MATTERS

People rarely begin with theological questions. They begin with personal ones:

"How do you stay hopeful?"
"How did you get through that?"
"What keeps you going?"

These questions reveal spiritual curiosity. They are not asking for an argument—they are asking for authenticity. They want to understand the hope they see taking shape in your life.

Peter tells us to "always be prepared to make a defense... for the hope that is in you" (1 Peter 3:15). That hope is not vague optimism or positive thinking—it is rooted in what we believe to be true about Jesus. Doctrine gives substance to our hope, but hope is often what people encounter first.

The six lines offer a simple way to make that hope visible— showing that it is not grounded in personality, resilience, or inner strength, but in the finished work of Christ.

And because the drawing is visual, it lowers defenses. It doesn't feel confrontational; it feels conversational. Truth is still being proclaimed, but it is carried by hope that can be seen, felt, and understood.

Often, that is all someone needs—to see hope clearly before they are ready to examine it more deeply.

WHEN YOU'RE TALKING WITH SOMEONE SKEPTICAL

Skepticism is often not rebellion—it is protection. For some, it grows out of genuine intellectual questions. For others, it is shaped by grief, disappointment, or wounds inflicted by churches or believers. And for many, it is a mixture of both— questions in the mind and pain in the heart.

Before explaining what you believe, it can be helpful to ask what they believe—and why. Listening honors their story. It communicates respect. And it often reveals that skepticism is less about rejecting God and more about trying to make sense of life as they have experienced it. When people feel heard, they are far more open to hearing.

When you say, "You don't have to agree with me; I just want to show you the story Christians believe," you shift the conversation from debate to invitation. You are not demanding agreement; you are offering understanding. You give them space to consider the gospel without pressure to accept it immediately.

The six lines help reframe Christianity—not as a list of rules or religious demands, but as a story that speaks to the deepest questions human beings carry, whether they call themselves skeptics or not:

Why is the world broken?
Why do humans long for more?
Why does guilt linger?
Why is forgiveness so difficult?
Why does death feel so wrong?

The gospel does not dismiss these questions. It names them. It enters them. And it responds—not abstractly, but personally, through the life, death, and resurrection of Jesus.

Often, that shift—from argument to story—is what opens the door.

WHEN YOU'RE SHARING ACROSS CULTURES OR RELIGIONS

Across cultures—Muslim, Hindu, Buddhist, animistic, secular, or atheist—brokenness is a shared reality. Every people group has its own language for sorrow, guilt, shame, fear, and longing. These experiences are universal because every human being is made in the image of God—and every image has been fractured.

This is why Paul's approach at Mars Hill (Acts 17) remains timeless. He began where people already were, acknowledged what they could recognize as true, and then pointed them toward Christ. He did not start with correction but with connection.

The six lines begin in the same way—with shared humanity. No one feels attacked or diminished when the conversation starts with brokenness. It is honest, universal, and disarming. From there, the cross reveals a God who comes near rather than a distant deity who demands performance. The final lines show a life shaped by love, not fear, obligation, or ritual.

This approach honors culture without compromising truth. It builds bridges rather than walls. And it trusts the Holy Spirit to do what no argument ever could.

WHEN YOU'RE TALKING WITH CHILDREN OR TEENS

Children love stories. Teenagers crave clarity. Both respond powerfully to pictures. The six lines give them something concrete—something they can see, remember, repeat, and share. The drawing helps them make sense of emotions they may not yet have words for: fear, shame, identity, belonging, purpose.

Young hearts understand the X because they encounter brokenness early in life. They respond to the cross because they long for rescue. They grasp the final lines because they desire meaning and direction. And when a child understands the gospel clearly, they often carry it with a purity and boldness that inspires the adults around them.

WHEN YOU HAVE TIME FOR A LONGER CONVERSATION

Not every conversation is brief, and not every heart opens quickly. Long conversations—on road trips, quiet walks, hospital waiting rooms, or shared meals—allow the gospel to unfold slowly, tenderly, and relationally.

In these moments, the six lines become a guide rather than a script. You draw at their pace. You listen more than you speak. You answer questions gently. You connect Scripture naturally. You allow silence to do some of the work.

Just as Jesus did not rush people, the gospel often moves most powerfully through presence before proclamation. In slower conversations, deeper wounds and longings surface—things that quick moments rarely reveal. Here, the gospel becomes not only clear, but compelling.

WHEN THE DOOR SEEMS CLOSED, THEN SUDDENLY OPENS

Some people appear uninterested until a single sentence slips out.

"I'm struggling."
"I feel lost."
"I'm overwhelmed."
"I don't know where to go from here."

Often, these words carry years of buried pain. When they surface, the heart is exposed—sometimes for the first time.

In moments like these, the gospel becomes a lifeline rather than a lesson. The six lines offer a gentle way to help someone name the ache they already feel (brokenness), see God's love moving toward them (the cross), and imagine a different future shaped by grace (the final lines).

Hearts often open slowly—and then all at once.

WHEN YOU'RE HELPING A NEW BELIEVER GROW

This drawing is not only for sharing the gospel; it is also a pathway for discipleship. New believers learn to understand:

Brokenness — the world's story and their own

Redemption — what Jesus has done and why it matters

Worship — the new life they now live in Him

The six lines form a framework for teaching, counseling, parenting, mentoring, and small-group life. They anchor new believers in the essentials while empowering them to share their hope with others—often sooner than they think they're ready.

This is what happened with Revocatus on Maisome Island. He believed the gospel in the morning, and by afternoon, he was pointing others to the same hope he had just received. Redeemed people naturally become messengers.

A FINAL WORD

Every conversation is different. Every heart opens differently. Every moment invites its own kind of response. But the gospel is spacious enough and strong enough to enter any context. The six lines simply give you a way to carry it with clarity.

You don't need eloquence.
You don't need a stage.
You don't need perfect timing.

You need a willing heart, a listening ear, and the courage to ask, "Can I show you something simple?"

The Holy Spirit will take it from there.

—

PART VI

THE MISSION &
THE URGENCY

SOMEONE IS WAITING

The islands scattered across Lake Victoria in Tanzania are places where beauty and brokenness rest side by side. The lake is enormous and unpredictable—its waters brown and restless, stirred constantly by fishing boats, daily work, and the weight of life lived close to the margins. Smoke rises from small cooking fires. Children run barefoot across rocky ground. Fishermen mend their nets while listening for sudden storms that can change everything. Life here feels rugged, raw, and honest.

Not every island is the same, but many carry a deep spiritual heaviness. For generations, witchcraft and fear have shaped daily life in some communities. Witchdoctors guide decisions. Rituals determine protection and prosperity. Darkness weaves itself quietly into the rhythms of everyday existence, shaping how families interpret sickness, safety, belonging, and the future.

A few years ago, my team and I traveled to one of these islands to encourage a small group of believers. Shortly after we arrived, I received word that a respected elder, Mzee Yohana, wanted to speak with me. In Swahili, Mzee is a title of honor—something like calling someone "sir" or "elder." I assumed he had questions about our presence on the island. But God had prepared something far weightier, something I would never forget.

After greeting each other, we talked for a while about his people, their challenges, and the questions he carried with him. As he spoke, I sensed the Holy Spirit gently prompting me to shift from conversation to proclamation. So I began to share the gospel—starting with brokenness, explaining that the world is not the way God created it to be and that sin has fractured everything around us and within us. Yohana listened carefully. His eyes were fixed. His posture was open. Something in him was searching.

Then I moved to the cross.

I told him clearly that Jesus is the perfect and final sacrifice—that His blood brings forgiveness, breaks the power of darkness, and ends the need for any other offering. As I spoke, I sensed a heaviness in my spirit, urging me to linger there. So I repeated it, and then again, each time with deeper clarity: the sacrifice of Jesus is sufficient. His blood is enough. Nothing else is needed. No other sacrifice is required.

As the words settled, Yohana's expression began to change. His face tightened. His eyes filled with a mixture of pain and awakening. It felt as though truth was pushing its way into places long shrouded in fear.

Suddenly, he rose, gripped my arm, and said quietly, "Come. I must show you something."

He led me behind his home to a small, freshly dug grave. The soil was still soft. The ground was unsettled—the air heavy with the scent of earth and grief.

With a trembling voice, he said, "If you had come one week earlier with this message, I would not have given my son's blood to the witchdoctors. They told me his sacrifice was required to protect me and bring prosperity."

My heart sank as the truth hit me with crushing weight.

A father.
A grave.
A son.

A lie demanding blood.
Darkness swallowing hope.
A gospel that had not reached him in time.

I could not hold back tears. Standing beside that grave, I felt a weight I had never carried before. This was not a theological abstraction—it was a human story, a father's unimaginable loss, a picture of what spiritual blindness produces when truth has not yet arrived.

Then the Holy Spirit impressed something on my heart with a clarity I have never been able to escape:

People are not only broken. They are spiritually dying.

Not because they have rejected Jesus—but because they have never heard who He truly is.

There are countless "Yohanas" in this world—people living under burdens Christ has already lifted, carrying fears Christ has already silenced, performing sacrifices Christ has already fulfilled. Many live in chains Christ has already broken. Many suffer under lies Christ has already defeated.

That day, Yohana surrendered his life to Jesus. His repentance was deep. His relief was visible. He saw the difference between the cruel demands of darkness and the love of a Savior who offered Himself in his place.

But even in his salvation, one truth remained: The gospel had reached him too late to save his son.

I left the island with a holy ache—an ache that clarified my calling and rearranged my priorities. It was the moment I understood with absolute clarity:

The best time to share the gospel is never "later."
It is always now (2 Corinthians 6:2).

And this is why it matters.

THE REALITY OF ETERNITY

Standing beside that grave confronted me with the truth Scripture has spoken from the beginning: eternity is certain. Hebrews 9:27 declares, "It is appointed for man to die once, and after that comes judgment." Every person—whether on a remote island or in a busy city—carries an eternal soul.

Paul says we were "dead in our trespasses and sins" (Ephesians 2:1). Without Christ, spiritual death is the condition of humanity. Eternity is not a theory; it is the destination of every single life. This is why the gospel cannot wait. Because eternity does not wait.

THE PRESENCE OF SPIRITUAL DARKNESS

Darkness is not simply a cultural phenomenon. It is a spiritual kingdom (Colossians 1:13). On Lake Victoria's islands, darkness manifests in rituals and sacrifices. In other parts of the world, it appears as addiction, pride, shame, materialism, anxiety, or the quiet emptiness no success can erase.

Jesus said, "The thief comes only to steal and kill and destroy" (John 10:10). Darkness steals dignity, destroys families, blinds hearts—and it does not leave by accident.

Only the gospel breaks darkness. This is why the message is urgent. Because darkness is active—and only Christ defeats it.

THE SUFFICIENCY OF CHRIST'S REDEMPTION

At the heart of the Christian faith is substitution: Jesus in our place.

Paul writes, "For our sake He made Him to be sin who knew no sin, so that in Him we might become the righteousness of God" (2 Corinthians 5:21). When Jesus declared, "It is finished" (John 19:30), He proclaimed that salvation was fully accomplished. No other sacrifice is required.

No more rituals.
No more blood.
No more attempts to earn what Christ has already provided.

This is why the gospel must be spoken. Because many are still carrying burdens Christ has already borne.

THE MISSION CHRIST HAS GIVEN US

Jesus entrusted His message to ordinary people—not angels,
not experts, not professionals. He said, "Make disciples of
all nations" (Matthew 28:19). He promised, "You will be my
witnesses… to the end of the earth" (Acts 1:8).

The gospel reached you because someone obeyed. It will reach
others because you choose to obey. God has no backup plan for
reaching the world. You are His plan.

This truth is not a burden; it is an invitation to purpose.

THE POWER OF SIMPLICITY

Paul summarized the gospel in a few sentences (1 Corinthians
15:3–4). Jesus used simple pictures—seeds, lamps, fields, bread.
The early church carried the message across continents without
complex strategies.

Clarity multiplies. Complexity paralyzes.

This is why the six lines matter—not because the tool is
special, but because the message is simple enough for anyone
to share, anywhere.

Six strokes.
Three symbols.
One Savior.
One story.

Simplicity makes the gospel accessible. Accessibility makes the gospel unstoppable.

THE INVITATION TO BE USED BY GOD

Someone in your life is already waiting.

A coworker hiding exhaustion behind humor. A neighbor quietly unraveling. A relative who has heard about church but never heard the gospel clearly. A friend weighed down by shame. A stranger you may meet only once. A man on an island who waited one week too long.

Scripture calls us "ambassadors for Christ" (2 Corinthians 5:20). We do not carry our own message; we carry His. And we do not step into random moments—we walk into works God has already prepared. "We are his workmanship, created in Christ Jesus for good works, which God prepared beforehand, that we should walk in them" (Ephesians 2:10).

You are not where you are by accident.

Your workplace, your neighborhood, your relationships, your daily rhythms—even the interruptions—are spaces where God intends to make His light visible through a willing life.

You were saved for more than survival, redeemed for more than comfort, and forgiven for more than personal peace. You were entrusted with hope—hope meant to be carried.

We do not know how long a door will remain open in someone's heart. We do not control another person's timeline. But we do know this: the opportunity before us is real, and the gospel is urgent.

The urgency of the gospel rests on four unchanging realities:

> » Eternity is certain, and every person you meet is moving toward it.

> » Darkness is active, and only the light of Christ breaks its power.

> » Jesus has finished the work of redemption, and His salvation is available today.

> » And God has chosen to carry His message through ordinary believers, filling willing lives with extraordinary hope.

These truths remind us that the gospel cannot wait for a more convenient moment—because eternity, darkness, Christ's victory, and our calling are all real right now.

The best time to share the gospel is not someday, when we feel more prepared or when life feels less complicated. It is today—while the conversation is still possible, while the heart is still listening, while someone is still waiting.

A PRAYER AND A COMMISSION

There are moments in our walk with God that feel less like turning a page and more like stepping onto holy ground. This final chapter is one of those moments. You have walked through the six lines, felt the weight of the story they tell, and seen the heart of God revealed in every stroke. Now, you stand at the edge of something sacred—a moment where understanding becomes obedience, where the gospel moves from your heart into the world around you.

You were not redeemed merely to be rescued.
You were redeemed to be sent.

Jesus said, "As the Father has sent Me, even so I am sending you" (John 20:21). This calling is not a burden but an invitation to join in God's mission. The One who sought you now sends you. The One who saved you now equips you. The One who restored you now invites you to join Him in His work across the world.

And if you feel unqualified or unprepared, you are standing exactly where countless followers of Jesus have stood before you.

I did not feel qualified when God saved me at fourteen. I did not feel prepared when I first preached in Tanzania's villages. I did not feel equipped when I was arrested in Ujiji. But qualification was never God's requirement.

Willingness was.

And willingness—offered in faith—has always been enough for Him.

THE COST OF THE CALLING

The gospel is good news, but carrying it is not always comfortable. Scripture never hides this. Jesus said, "If anyone would come after Me, let him deny himself, take up his cross, and follow Me" (Mark 8:34). The apostles echoed this with their lives (Acts 5:41; 2 Timothy 3:12).

The cross does not merely save us—it shapes us.

Some costs are small: awkward conversations, rejection, and inconvenience. Others are heavier. But every believer will face moments when following Jesus costs something—comfort, pride, time, reputation, or control.

I learned this in ways I never expected. In 2009, a few months after my release from prison in Ujiji—where God confronted my unforgiveness toward my father—I traveled to Kondoa, a central region of Tanzania with a strong Muslim presence.

Sharing the gospel there was difficult. Some local religious leaders opposed our work, including a man named Yahya. Yahya was an imam—a spiritual leader and teacher within the local mosque. He was highly respected, deeply sincere in his faith, and determined to protect his community from what he believed was dangerous teaching. He encouraged young men from their madrasa—their Islamic religious school—to chase us away with stones whenever we preached. Tension rose quickly.

One morning, while I was on a prayer walk, Yahya approached me alone. This time, he carried a knife.

"Yusuph," he said, "we have tried everything to make you leave. Today, in the name of Allah, I am going to kill you. This is our act of worship."

His voice was steady. His eyes were hard. And he meant every word. He stepped forward, raised the knife, and drove it toward my chest. By God's mercy, he missed my heart, but the blade sliced deeply between my fingers. Blood poured down my hand.

Fear surged—but something deeper held me still.

Yahya hesitated. My lack of resistance confused him. "Why are you not defending yourself?" he asked.

What came out of my mouth next was not rehearsed. It was the Holy Spirit speaking through me.

"Yahya," I said, "you serve your god, and I serve mine. Your god asks you to defend him by killing me. My God does not need me to defend Him—He stands alone. Whatever you choose today, my God commands me to love you. You could kill me now, and if you repent tomorrow and follow Jesus, you will be my brother in Christ, and we will stand together in heaven."

He froze. His face changed. Then slowly, he lowered the knife, shook his head, and walked away.

Our time in Kondoa ended soon after, but the Holy Spirit kept pressing one message into my heart: *Go back.* Every logical thought in me protested. But obedience rose stronger than fear.

When I finally returned, the first person I met was Yahya. This time, there was no knife. Only questions. Real, searching questions.

"Where do you get this confidence in your faith?" he asked.

That simple question opened the door to a long conversation shaped by humility and hunger for truth. Before the day was over, Yahya surrendered his life to Jesus Christ. The man who once sought to take my life found eternal life in the Savior who had spared mine.

Stories like this are rare, but the principles behind them are not. Every follower of Jesus will encounter moments where love requires courage and obedience comes with a cost. Whether small or great, Christ is worthy.

Yahya's story is not mainly about danger or deliverance. It is a picture of what it means to follow Jesus in the real world.

This is where the gospel becomes mission.
Where belief becomes obedience.
Where the story becomes calling—not just mine, but yours.

You were saved for this.
You were shaped for this.
You were sent for this.

And the God who calls you promises to go with you to the end of the age (Matthew 28:20).

THE PRAYER

Father,

Thank You for this beloved one who has journeyed through these pages.

Thank You for redeeming them, shaping them, and drawing them into Your story.

Strengthen their heart with holy courage.

Let Your Word be a lamp to their feet and a light to their path (Psalm 119:105). Let Your love be the power that compels them (2 Corinthians 5:14).

Open doors that no one else can open. Close doors not meant for them. Grant them moments where heaven touches the ordinary— moments prepared by Your Spirit and filled with Your presence.

When fear whispers, remind them You are near (Isaiah 41:10). When doubt rises, remind them You have chosen them (John 15:16). When opportunities come, remind them You speak through willing vessels.

Empower their steps.
Anoint their words.
Guard their heart.

Let their lives reflect the beauty of Jesus wherever You send them.

Amen.

THE COMMISSION

Now, in the name of Jesus Christ—the Savior who rescued you, redeemed you, and now sends you—receive this commission:

Go into your world with humility and courage.

Go with the compassion of Christ and the power of the Spirit.

Go with love that listens, truth that saves, and hope that endures.

Go knowing that God has gone before you—that every conversation, every encounter, every step is already held in His sovereign hands.

Go, because someone is waiting.

And as you go, take heart:
The Savior who sends you walks beside you, goes before you,and will be with you always—to the end of the age (Matthew 28:20).

To God be the glory—
in your life,
in your steps,
and in the stories yet to unfold.

—

TOOLS TO LEARN, REMEMBER, AND SHARE THE SIX LINES

THE 6 LINES

VISUAL DIAGRAM

BROKENNESS   **REDEMPTION**   **WORSHIP**

HOW TO DRAW IN 3 EASY STEPS

STEP 1:	STEP 2:	STEP 3:
Draw an X	**Draw a cross**	**Draw upward & outward lines**

"Life is broken—around us and within us."

"Jesus stepped into our brokenness to rescue us."

"When we trust Him, He gives us a new direction: upward and outward."

Six lines.
Three movements.
One story.
One Savior.

QUICK REFERENCE GUIDE

3 MOVEMENTS OF THE SIX LINES

BROKENNESS:
The world is broken—and so are we. Sin has separated us from God.

SAY: "Our world is beautiful, but it's broken—and that brokenness lives in us too."

SCRIPTURE: Romans 3:23

REDEMPTION:
God did not leave us in our brokenness. Jesus lived the life we could not live, died the death we deserved, and rose again to bring us back to God.

SAY: "Jesus stepped into our brokenness to forgive us and restore us."

PAUSE here to invite response

"God invites us to turn from sin and trust Jesus. Would you like to receive His forgiveness and follow Him today?"

If they're ready, PRAY together.

SCRIPTURE: John 3:16, Romans 5:8, Romans 10:9

WORSHIP:
When we trust Jesus, He gives us a new direction: Love God (↑) and love others (→).

SAY: "When Jesus saves us, He gives us a new way to live—loving God and loving others in response to His grace."

SCRIPTURE: Matthew 22:37–39